Revocable Trust Reit

A Pocket Guide to Creating a Living Revocable Trust

(The Truth About Revocable Living Trusts and Estate Planning)

Loretta Kerns

Published By **Loretta Kerns**

Loretta Kerns

All Rights Reserved

*Retirement Planning: The Brief Guide to Lifelong Financial
Freedom (Retirement Planning Guide for Dummies and
How to Make Your Money Last)*

ISBN 978-1-77485-445-7

ISBN 978-1-77485-445-7

Legal & Disclaimer

The information contained in this book is not designed to replace or take the place of any form of medicine or professional medical advice. The information in this book has been provided for educational and entertainment purposes only.

The information contained in this book has been compiled from sources deemed reliable, and it is accurate to the best of the Author's knowledge; however, the Author cannot guarantee its accuracy and validity and cannot be held liable for any errors or omissions. Changes are periodically made to this book. You must consult your doctor or get professional medical advice before using any of the suggested remedies, techniques, or information in this book.

Upon using the information contained in this book, you agree to hold harmless the Author from and against any damages, costs, and expenses, including any legal fees potentially resulting from the application of any of the

TABLE OF CONTENTS

Introduction

There is no best time in one's lifetime to start planning for your estate and your heirs. As people approach retirement, many begin to plan for the future. Many would argue this is too late. Although it is true you should start planning for retirement as early as possible, you should also create an Estate Plan to protect your loved and hard-earned assets.

Estate Planning is not something most people believe applies to them. They are not wealthy. They don't own multiple houses, numerous stocks, or vast personal wealth. This is a mistake. Estate Planning is something everyone should do. Estate Planning protects you assets, regardless how big or small. Estate Planning makes it simpler for your heirs and beneficiaries to manage the transfer, regardless how large or small the assets. Estate planning eases the burdens of your family when you are grieving the loss of a loved person. Estate

1

Planning can be accomplished using many tools. Researching to fully understand your options is important and consulting a professional is always a wise move.

A Living Trust can be a legal document you create to oversee the transfer and administration of your assets. The main point is that the Living Trust is created during your life and has an impact in how your assets are dealt with while you are still living. A review of the following information about Living Trusts is a part of your Estate Planning research. This includes but is not limited to: Who should have a Living Trust? What property can and should be placed into a Living Trust? What is the difference between a Will or a Living Trust? Why should you avoid probate?

It is crucial that you plan for your life in the future. Many feel they don't have to, or that the planning can be postponed. You can't afford to wait any longer to protect your family. Living Trusts can be an important tool in reaching that goal.

Chapter 1: Wills Vs. Trusts - Difference

The easiest tool in your Estate Planning tools is the creation and execution of a Last Will. A large number of people believe that a Last Will and Testament is the only way you can transfer your assets on your death. This is false. Many Life Insurance policies provide beneficiaries. Beneficiaries are available for Individual Retirement Plans (IRAs/Roth IRAs, 401ks) A beneficiary can have some bank accounts held in Trust. Joint ownership of real estate or other property is possible with rights for survivorship. A Living Trust may be created.

Let's now look at a Last Will and Testament. This will show you what property will follow the will. A will can be legally created. It must be witnessed at the witness of two witnesses. The will must notarized in public. In your Will, you designate an Executor to take care of your assets when you die. An Executor can be considered a fiduciary. He is required to act in the best interests the Estate.

You can set where certain assets, such as personal property, stocks or bonds, will be distributed. As long as the other instruments do not supersede the will, you are able to. Let us examine real estate. Married couples often purchase real estate together. They share the ownership of the property, which gives them rights of survivorship. This means that your spouse's property ownership will transfer to you automatically when they pass away. You don't need to appoint an Executor, nor do the courts have to get involved. Probate is the procedure we'll be discussing later. If you are the sole owner, you will need a legal document such as a will to transfer the property.

Others assets can be transferred to beneficiaries, such life insurance, bank accounts, IRAs or 401ks. If you have already named a beneficiary, your property will be automatically transferred to the beneficiary upon your death.

Finally, there's a Living Trust. Living Trusts are similar to Wills in that they must be executed, signed and witnessed by you in front of witnesses. It is a legally binding instrument. It can be either irrevocable oder revocable. Living Trusts tend to be revocable. That means you can change the Trust at any time in your life. A Living Trust is composed of three components. They include the Trustee, the grantor, and the beneficiary. The grantor creates the Trust. He or she also transfers property into the Living Trust. The Trustee oversees all property that is included in the Trust. After you die, the Trustee can grant the property to the beneficiary.

You will usually appoint yourself as the initial Trustee for a Living Trust. This allows you to retain control of the Trust throughout your lifetime. As long your capacity allows you to modify, amend or change the Trust, or even revoke it. Once you die, the Trust document names a successor Trustee. This makes the Trust irrevocable. The Trust document is irrevocable after your death.

You can transfer any and everything you own to the Trust after it is established. You can move real estate both in-state as well out of state. Additionally, you can transfer bank account balances and personal property. You must consider whether the property has an existing automatic ownership transfer mechanism before you transfer it to a Trust. Does your joint ownership of any real property, such as real estate, make it a joint owner? Are there named beneficiaries on any IRAs or life policies? This will eliminate the need for the Trust to hold the property.

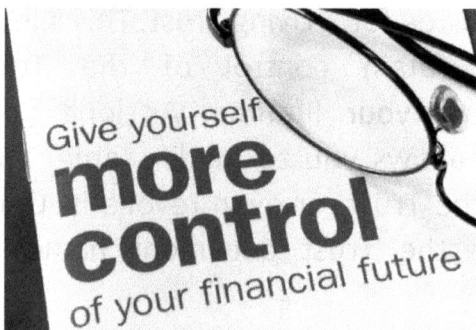

Give yourself **more control** of your financial future

While you're alive, you can legally still own the property legally transferred to Trust. You are the Trustee and can do anything you wish with the property. It is yours to keep, sell, invest, or gift it to someone else. It can be used as a single entity, but it cannot be subject to any tax forms or fees. The Living Trust becomes active upon your death.

A Living Trust and Last Will and Testament perform the exact same legal function. The main difference is that after your death, a Will must be submitted before a Living Trust can take effect. This gives the successor Trustee the power to collect and disburse Trust property. This saves time and energy as well the high fees and costs of Probate, and goes through the Court system. This is one way you can lessen the burden for your family during the difficult period after your passing. Even if you choose to establish a Living Trust for your loved ones, it is always good to have a second Last Will and Testament.

Chapter 2: Who Wont Have A Living Truth?

Before you choose the tools you need to create your Estate Plan you should consider whether you require a Living Trust or a Last Will and Testament. Of course, the easiest choice is to do nothing. However, that's never a good option. It comes with its own set of problems and headaches. In order to ensure that assets are transferred to your heirs upon your death, you will need to have a Will, Living Trust, or other legal instrument in place. The court must appoint someone to manage your Estate. The administrator acts without the need for a will and functions as an executor. The Administrator must collect all of your property assets and make your payments. Finally, they will distribute the assets according a law that is different from your wishes. This process will take many months and also add costs, fees, charges, and additional expenses to the estate. While doing nothing is the easiest way to go for now, it's not the best choice because of all the problems it causes after your death.

There are many things to consider when you decide if a Living Trust should be chosen. Living Trusts are designed to prevent Probate, reduce stress, help with costs, and provide financial support for your family. First, a Living Trust might not work for you if the person you are is young and healthy. A Will is more straightforward to create. There is less need to worry about probate fees at this stage of your life because you are more likely to die. It may be possible to avoid probate costs by using other methods as you get older. The ability to name a beneficiary in any securities you have means that the securities can be transferred to probate. Even though a Living Trust seems inconvenient and unnecessary for young people, it can provide protection against unexpected illness or death.

Minor children are more concerned with their financial welfare and well-being than anyone else. When you want to appoint a guardian or financial support for your children's upbringing, a Will will be the right tool. A Life Insurance policy can also be used to help with financial worries for your minor kids.

Another important factor is whether property is held jointly. Any jointly owned real property automatically transfers your interest to the survivor if you are deceased. A Living Trust is not necessary for jointly held property. Bank accounts held jointly by joint owners become solely the property of the survivor upon your death.

Your estate size and assets are important. If your estate is worth millions, you'll want to avoid probate costs. Additionally, you will want to be the sole judge of how and where your hard-earned money is distributed. It is also important to determine the asset type. Whether you are an owner of a small or large business, you don't want interruptions in the management and you don't want your business interests tied up in probate.

All these factors need to be taken into account when deciding if Living Trusts are right for you. It is a good idea to at least think about Estate Planning. Living Trusts may be beneficial for you. If you own property or have an extensive estate, it is important to assess your individual situation and determine whether you need a Living Trust.

Chapter 3: Benefits A Living Trust

As mentioned, a Living Trust could be a valuable tool for you to achieve your Estate Planning goals. Living Trusts can be distinguished from Last Will and Testaments by the ability to transfer assets and property without the need of court involvement. This helps to reduce the costs and fees associated in probate as well as the time required for the distribution of the property. California Law recently made it mandatory for Trust documents to be communicated by written notices. Even with this additional time, a Living Trust may be processed and property distributed within 6-8months, while probate takes up to 20months and can cost substantially higher.

A Living Trust can also be used to protect out-of-state property. If you have a second residence, vacation home, condominium, or other property in another state, a Will must be filed and a probate proceeding initiated in that particular state. This means that you will have to pay twice as much, pay double the fees and go through double the hassles. A Living Trust is recognized as a valid legal document in most states. This allows you to transfer ownership of property or assets. As such, out of-state property can be handled as all other property within the Living Trust.

As we already discussed, younger, healthy individuals are less likely be in need of a Living Trust. Living Trusts have a significant benefit for both seniors and younger individuals. A conservatorship is where an individual petitions the court to name them as conservator for an individual's finances, in the case of a person becoming mentally or physically incapable. Conservatorships are costly, disruptive, and can take a lot of time for all involved.

A Living Trust allows for you to designate a successor Trustee if you are unable to carry out your day-to-day affairs due to any type of illness or impairment. The Trust property will be managed by the successor Trustee who can make use of it to the benefit of the grantor. This allows for easy handling of all financial matters. This is not something that happens only to the elderly. Many times, tragedy strikes young people leaving them unable or unable to do their daily tasks. It is always safer to be safe than sorry.

The Living Trust is not registered with any court or other individual. This means that your Estate Plan is kept secret and confidential. This may not seem like much, but it is important for someone with a large estate who has many assets. They remain your business. Your choice about how to distribute hard earned assets is up to you. Although certain states require Living Trusts to be registered in order to protect their assets, the majority of states will only require you to file paperwork proving the Trust exists. California does not currently require the filing of such paperwork. California law requires all potential beneficiaries to be informed of the Living Trust. If they do not wish to contest it, they can. The information will be restricted to a very select number of individuals.

You retain full control of all of your assets over the course your lifetime. You have complete control over all of your assets. The Trust is able to allow you to add or take out property. You can cancel the Trust at any moment. The Living Trust's creation does not impact your ability to control, distribute, and manage your assets during your lifetime. You don't need to treat the Trust separately for tax purposes. There is no need to declare the Trust's interest as a separate entity. The Living Trust is exempt from the usual recordkeeping requirements that are required for transfer of certain types property. To manage your Trust property, you can name any person that you have faith in. No lawyer is required to distribute Trust property.

A Living Trust is not without its merits. They do NOT reduce state estate taxes. Federal estate tax exemptions, currently $5,000,000, are adopted by most states. This means that, unless your estate exceeds $5million dollars, you will not need to pay any estate taxes, regardless of whether or not there is a Living Trust. A Living Trust is not able to exempt your estate from any taxes above $5,000,000.

The paperwork is often more complex than a Last Will. You should ensure that all property and assets are legally transferred into the Trust. All creditors will have a claim on any outstanding debt, regardless if the Living Trust is in existence. Some financial institutions might be reluctant or unable to lend money or make a mortgage on the property once it is legally owned by the Trust. In some states, transfer tax may be charged for property transfers into Trusts. California does away with this. The transfer tax you pay to convert your ownership to the Living Trust is not applicable. If you are considering whether a Living Trust might be right for yourself, you should weigh all of its benefits and drawbacks in relation to your circumstances.

Chapter 4: Probate, What Is It And Why Should I Choose To Avoid?

The Living Trust and Last Will and Testament are different in that they avoid probate. Probate is the process through which assets of an Estate can be approved by the Court to be distributed by either an Executor of Last Will and Testament or an Administrator of a court created estate. Both the Administrator and executor perform the same function during probate. They act as fiduciaries for the Estate's best interests. The Last Will, Testament and wishes of the deceased must be respected by the executor. Each state's laws will govern who is entitled to receive property. The Executor is a combination of the two.

The process of probate begins when the potential Executor files an application in court for appointment as Executor. Most often, the Executor hires an attorney to handle the legal paperwork. The petition tells the court information such as the amount of the estate, beneficiaries and heirs involved, and also the name and address of the petitioner. A court paralegal looks over the paperwork to determine if an Executor can be appointed under state law. These appointments are typically routine, unless there are objections. The paperwork will need to be approved by the Judge in charge of the case. This is not always possible. A court hearing may be required in certain cases, such as if there is a contest. This will add more time and expense to the probate process.

Once the Judge has approved that the Executor be appointed, letters of testamentary or letters of administration are issued. These letters allow the Executor act as the legal representative for the estate and are able to perform all legal duties. Once appointed, the Executor must inventory all estate assets. The Executor must make sure that all assets are appraised to their fair market value. He must pay all outstanding monetary and funeral expenses debts. He may sell some of the assets in order to pay these obligations. The Executor must maintain detailed records and file all required forms for taxes. Once these steps are completed and approved by the court, the Executor may file another petition asking permission to distribute the assets. The executor may begin to divide the property according the Last Will & Testament once the Judge has approved it. Be aware, however, that distributions of property during probate proceedings are not allowed unless approved by the court.

Probate for most estates is a waste. Distributions are made within a small circle of friends and family. There are no objections or contests to either the Last Will and Testament or to the administration. The probate process takes between 12-20 month if everything runs smoothly. However, it may take longer if there are more assets to transfer or have complicated procedures.

The main concern with probate is the costs and fees associated with it. Each state sets its own fees and guidelines for the Administrator, Executor and Attorney involved in the legal process. The fees are usually related with the gross estate being dealt with. The gross property includes all assets which are likely to be affected by the administration of or probate. Other assets that go beyond the probate process are not included, such life insurance policies, IRA beneficiaries, or Living Trusts.

California Probate Code governs these proceedings. The original filing charge for the petition is $435. Other costs that may be associated with the petition include appraisal fees, a probate referee who will determine fair market values, publication of notices costs, as well as costs for certified court documents and the issuance the letters. The Executor and Attorney account for the greatest costs. These are governed California Probate Code Section 10810 (which is entirely dependent on the gross property). The Attorney and Executor each get the same compensation for their duties. In extraordinary cases, the Executor or Attorney may petition the court for additional fees.

The code allows for a 4 percent fee for the first $100,000.00; 3 percent for the next $100,000.00; 2 percent on the next $800,000.00; 1 percent on the next 9,000,000.00; 1/5 of next $15,000,000.00. All amounts above $25,000,000.00 require court approval. If the gross estate is

$100,000.00 the total fees would be $8,000.00. This includes $4,000.00 per Attorney and $4,000.00 per Executor.

Estate Valuation and Estimate Fees:

Value $200,000 Fees $14,000

Value $300,000.

Value $500,000 Fees $36,000

Value $750,000 Fees $36,000

Value $1,000,000 Fees $46,000

This is the major reason why we want to avoid probate. It is not limited to the wealthy. While a $200,000.00 estate is not excessively expensive, $14,000.00 per year in fees is still significant when you consider the potential filing fees and court cost.

Probate is an involved and complex process. To complete the paperwork required, you need to hire an attorney. The Executor must be detail-oriented, attentive to facts and a good listener. You should hope everything goes smoothly with court. The court process can take up to a year, is expensive and can cause headaches for your family.

Chapter 5: How Renting Property Will Make It Easier To Retire Than Investing In Bonds

When people look at the differences between the bond and rental markets, they often have trouble understanding why it is better to focus your efforts on rental properties. This chapter will highlight the advantages and disadvantages of renting properties, while explaining why they are better than bonds. We will begin by explaining the difference between renting property and bonds. This will help to clarify why one is better. Which one provides better cash flow? This is important if your goal is to retire early and be able to retire.

The bond markets are essentially made up of other markets. The bond market is made up of three markets:

1. The corporate

2. The treasury

3. The municipal

The yields and price movements are not the same. You also need to consider the spreads as well as the duration. What a bond does is provide security. It is a security that will pay a fixed amount to the holder. They do this at a regular time for the holder. A bond is a type of debt security. The investors are called lenders and the issuers borrowers. Markets are those that move when there is an expectation for economic growth.

An investment in rental property and property rentals is the purchase of real estate with the intention and expectation of receiving a return. This could be by selling the property or renting it to other people. There are two options. Flipping is the other option. You have bought an asset that you want to sell for quick profits instead of it gaining value over time. You can either sell it immediately or let it appreciate over the long term to earn a return.

Now that we have explained the differences between the two, it is possible to explain why rental investing makes more sense. Renting in real estate gives you greater control than stocks and bonds. Each property you purchase, whether it is physical or virtual, puts you in complete control. It places you in the office of a

CEO. As a CEO, it will allow you to reduce investment costs and to make improvements.

You'll be able rent increase or to find better tenants if you have the right tenants. Also, you'll be in a position to make the most of the market. The downside to this is that the economic cycle can still affect you. Overall, however, rental properties give you more control over making the right decisions to maximize your wealth. Investors in public or private companies are called minority investors. You have to believe in management. This can have its disadvantages. For example, managers may commit fraud or make poor decisions that lead to the company's failure. This is a very important point to remember. No one cares more than you about your investments. Physical investments can also be better for you.

Another benefit is what's called leverage. If there is a rising stock market, leverage can be an asset. Even if real property only tracks inflation over a certain period of time, the results will still be there. This makes it easier to understand. For example, let's suppose that there is an increase in inflation of 3% over the long term. This means that if 20% of your deposit is made, then you can expect a 15% profit. This is known to be a cash on return.

This means that in five years, you will have effectively doubled your equity. Stocks produce about 9% annually, including dividends. Leverage can lead to a steep decline in value, so make sure you consider the worst case scenarios before you invest. This example shows how property is more desirable than investing.

Real estate is a tangible investment. It's something tangible that you can benefit from and something you can see with your own eye. Stocks or bonds are no longer just on paper. This does not offer comfort and doesn't work in your favor long term. You can think of it as this. It is important to have a place to turn to in the event of an emergency. This gives you more advantages.

A second benefit is the lower volatility. Even though your house value could drop, the utility and use of your home might not. If this happens, you can look at it from a completely different perspective and still make the most of the property. It's easy to see this by visualizing yourself at your computer screen or TV. It's possible to get upset by the facts, but it won't be as volatile if you don't. Even if there are some issues with your investment or how it's going, your investment will be less volatile than any other avenues.

We'll show you why investing in real estate is better than stocks and bonds. Last year, interest on your primary property can be deducted from your mortgage indebtedness up to $700,000. In certain cases, this is at least $50,000 more. You can also sell your primary home tax-free, up to $500,000, if you are married and have lived there for at least two years. Your tax-free profits could reach $250,000.

This will help you determine where you fall in the tax bracket. It's another reason to own property. If your tax bracket is greater than 28%, it is highly recommended you purchase property. It is also worth noting that your expenses for managing your properties are deductable from your income. However, there is one caveat. Income limits are still in effect. This means that you should not make more than $164,000 in a given year. And in some cases, $2,000 higher.

Real estate is also simpler to quantify and analyse. It is believed that you only need to be able calculate rental income and expenses in order to value a piece. Let's take as an example borrowing at 3%. If you have borrowed 3% and rented the property out for a yield of 6%+, then you are most likely a winner. Many people consider real estate a profitable field. However, you must have the finances and money to invest in it. An investor can build his wealth by focusing on the cash flow as well and the underlying equity.

This is different from stock because you have to believe what companies are reporting. Companies can alter numbers in many ways to make them look better. Companies can adjust receivables too. Companies can use different depreciation strategies and add one of their gains, or even different types of amortization. However, it is so much easier to do research on actual real property than stock and bond research. Zillow provides a great example. Zillow is an online marketplace that has been in use for more than a decade. This makes it one of my favorite places to look when looking to buy or rent a house. You will find the most up-to-date estimates and sales history as well as comparables, which makes it easier for you to do real estate research. There are street views and information about crime, so that you can answer all your questions.

The insulation of real estate is better than that of stocks and bonds. Real estate is generally more local for most people.

Most people know that unless someone is a millionaire, they won't be able to purchase real estate across the United States. That's what you can do, however. It will make you more resilient to the national and international economy if the region you choose to buy is economically strong. Brexit is an example. In fact, Brexit has helped to lower rates of mortgage as foreign investors bought bonds (US Treasury Bonds).

The so-called superstar cities, like New York, San Francisco or London, may show that they are the most resilient and are able gain the most. When investing in real property, it is important to understand that industries within your area may disappear very quickly and suddenly. This could leave you broke. Another tip is to diversify in lower-cost regions with higher yields to ensure that you are making the most out of this field. Many people use real estate crowdfunding in this venture.

Another reason why real estate is better for bonds is the possibility of getting a bailout if your mortgage is not paid. This includes tax-free points, mortgage interest taxes, and in recent years, the government took a more aggressive approach to going after banks. They have been successful in getting loan modifications extended. There are many states that aren't going after you if your mortgage is cancelled. California and Nevada, are two of them.

Real estate has its own advantages. It will help to understand these characteristics and determine if you are a good candidate for this field.

1. You should take pride and ownership. If you take pride in your property ownership, this can be a great benefit.

2. If you enjoy working with people. This can be a great opportunity to show others that you might prefer working as a part of a team.

3. If you're certain where it is, you should plan to live there for at most five years.

4. If you can't function well in a volatile setting.

5. If you believe in the real estate of wealth, it is not made of paper.

6. If you get easily scared off by downturns.

7. You might notice that you are buying and selling too frequently. Ironically, high transaction prices can discourage people from trading.

8. If you prefer to be more in control. Remember that stocks are often in the hands of other people and not yours. You have control over property and not the other.

It is best to have inflation-linked assistance. Crowdsourcing can also be a great option. Crowdsourcing companies might be a better option for you if you cannot afford the downpayment to purchase a property. Crowdsourcing can give you a diversified portfolio. You will be able to see the results of your efforts if it is well researched. When you examine the assets allocation mix of college endowment and high net worth individuals, you will see that real property weightings vary from 10% to 25%.

Crowdsourcing offers flexibility in real estate investment and investing. Crowdsourcing gives you the ability to invest anywhere you want, allowing you to achieve the highest possible returns. San Francisco is our example. The cap in this city is 3%. The cap rate for the Midwest is 3%. In the south, it's around 10%. If you're interested in this option, you'll see its special benefits.

Look around to find the best mortgage rates. You have many options. Lending Tree is a great example. Lending Tree is the largest network of lenders and has the highest competition for your business. Therefore, you should aim to get as much written offers as possible and then leverage these offers. This will ensure you receive the highest interest rate. Consider it this way: If you find a great deal and are able afford the payments, the property should be yours within ten-years. You should also try to secure low rates and neutral inflation.

It will also allow you to manage all of your finances in one location. This could also be a benefit in real estate. Online platforms are another option that you could use to manage your portfolio, finances, and other information. These online platforms will allow you to store everything in one place. You can also check on it frequently to make sure it's all correct. You must remember one thing: you shouldn't be over-optimistic. This doesn't help, and can lead to being overwhelmed and over-thinking.

Chapter 6: How Much You Will Need To Invest In Rental Property Properties

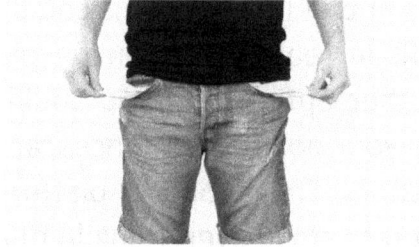

Many people worry about their money. People worry about money in every avenue. We are going give you accurate information you can use and will let you know how much to invest in your properties. It is clear that people often underestimate the amount of money they will need to make this happen. Some couples have believed that they would need millions of dollars to start this journey. This sounds unlikely, but research has shown that not all couples wait until they are rich to start this journey. People usually start out with one house before moving on to the next. Many people have received a single loan that was used to purchase a house. Then they rented it out for years and got another loan.

This is because so many people have different ideas. You need the right information. Let's begin. Money is a big issue for many. Our society is plagued by the inability to buy food, or even property. Many people are also responsible for paying bills, student loans, and taking care of their families. This means that many people won't be financially able for this profession. These tips will help if you don't have the means to pay for this degree or have other difficulties in your life.

Crowdfunding apps like Fundrise and crowd funding resources such as peer to peer loans or partnerships could help you invest less money in real property. This reduces the investment amount. This can reduce the cost of your investment by as much as $500 instead to more than $100,000. These are sites and apps that are quite new. Many people have not heard of them before.

Crowd funding apps, such as Fundrise, don't require you to deal with tenants or handle repairs. You can use Fundrise to invest in real-estate options. It is an online investment service that allows you put your money into a trust real estate investment trust. Instead, you can sit back and enjoy your money growing. These investments are popular because they offer excellent returns. The average return for this investment was over 10% in the last 2 years. Many people were shocked by this, as it's significantly higher than what you'll see in other investments. This app also allowed them to launch their crowdfunding platform without spending thousands of money. They don't offer a guarantee of a return on investment, but they have shown good results in the past. Fundraise is also easy to get involved in and you don't have to invest a lot. You can create a portfolio starting at $500. With as little money as $1000, you could get the income you want. You can invest with this platform for very low fees. There is a 0.85% management charge each year. This makes it a popular choice over other brokerages.

REIT can also be known as a real-estate investment trust. They are similar to mutual funds for realty. Larger stocks can be traded or kept in retirement accounts. A real-estate investment trust will typically invest in multiple properties. This could refer to buildings like retail space and apartment buildings, but could also be warehouses and other properties.

This might prove to be beneficial because it will give you the opportunity to either invest in commercial realty or large residential properties. You can be a shareholder instead of an investor with direct responsibility. These investments, if you're a limited partnership, are more like mutual money than any other things we've discussed. They are organized by a general partners who handle the management of all properties that are part of the partnership. This route will make it possible for all investors to be limited partners.

There are pros as well as cons to this investment and you should be aware. These are organized in such a manner that they can help you. When you invest in these the losses you incur are less than your actual investment. This is known by the term "limited liability". With only a few thousand dollars, you can invest in larger and more complicated real estate deals. This is great for beginners since you don't have to see all the details of complicated real property when you first start.

This is great news for those who don't have a lot of cash. However, this is very similar to owning stocks. As we have discussed in other chapters, stocks are not a good option. Or at most, not as good as investing on the property. It is possible to make a profit if your partnership has good management skills and invested in the successful deals. You could be able to receive a steady stream in dividends, which is much higher than what you get on stocks. Neglecting to manage a limited partnership can result in your entire investment being destroyed. You need a team with deep knowledge about real estate to manage a limited partner. These people would also be able teach you how to achieve consistent gains. This could make you very rich. Make sure you know what your team does.

We've already covered how owning a house can make you rich and how to get an appreciation in its price. It is possible to rent out your property as a rental property. We've talked about this before in other chapters. You can also invest in realty through peer to peer platforms. Crowd funding is often used to describe it. It allows you the opportunity to diversify relatively little money across multiple deals that you are able. There are new funds being made all the time through peer to peer crowd financing activities. Many people don't have enough cash to just buy a home. This is for people who are looking to invest in property.

Peer-to-peer platforms you may notice popping up everywhere you go are becoming more popular in the real world of investing. They are also based around real estate investing. Crowd financing is also known as this. This is when investors pool together their money for specific real-estate investments. This is a great way to make it easy for your friends and family. These platforms allow you to invest in property online via different types of realty, and in various ways.

Most people believe that purchasing properties is the only way they can get involved with real estate. But that is one of your biggest options. There are other ways you can invest. Make sure you research them all and get as much information as you can. This will enable you to choose the best method to increase your investment's return. Your investment will not be as liquid if it was invested in mutual fund or similar funds. The closest thing that you could compare it to is the ITS. With a peer to peer platform, you have more control over which deals to invest your money. The freedom to choose what you invest in is great. It makes you feel more in charge and allows you to make your own decisions, instead of depending on others. As we've said, diversifying your money through multiple deals gives you the chance to do so. It is possible to find new platforms all the time, which can help you gain a better insight into what you would like and which platform works best for your needs.

It's worth exploring commercial real estate. It might also be beneficial if your knowledge is good. It is a good idea to talk to your agent before you invest. They will be able to tell you about the benefits and best ways to go about it.

Be aware that commercial property is frequently the subject of business cycle. While many people aren't sure what this means, it's important to be aware. The business cycle and the observation of them mean that you must be alert to recessions and watch out for fluctuations. Your tenant may find it difficult to pay rent during a downturn in the economy. This is one of many reasons why commercial real estate investments should be avoided.

Flipping is another way to make money. There have been many TV shows that show people flipping houses. While this is a popular way to make money in property, it can also be very expensive. In order to buy a house, you will need to first fix it up. This is especially true in cases where the property requires extensive work. You should consider whether this investment is worth your money and time.

Here's an example. Let's imagine that you find $120,000 fixer upper. This will require you to pay $5,000 more in closing expenses. You want to make more on this property because that's what you have in mind. Although this is an excellent goal to have, it can be costly. In this example, you would need $50,000 to repair the property. This means that the property has been purchased for $175,000 For this house to be flipped, you will need someone who is willing and able to pay more. If you don't have the money, you will end up losing your money as well as your finances.

Even with all of the information mentioned above, you would still spend $145,000 dollars. It means that you will have to find someone who is willing pay that much to buy a house.

We have already shown you how to invest in different ways and what you could invest in for less money. Now we are going to show you the cheapest options. It means that, since the 1950s, as real estate became more popular in America, there have been less expensive ways to learn how to do this. You don't even have to spend a lot if money is tight.

For instance, in 1960s America the cheapest way for realty investors to participate in commercial property was to purchase the REIT mentioned earlier. The

REITs are the easiest and most affordable way to add property to your portfolio.

Everyone wanted a portfolio. Obviously, this is how investors see them. This was the beginning of being a serial investee. Securities can trade on major exchanges such as stocks or direct investment in real property. This is possible through property or mortgage investment. Some of these REITs can only invest in one particular area of real-estate, while others may invest only in a single geographic area.

High dividend distributions are exchanged for special tax considerations. REITs also provide a highly liquid means of investing in real estate. This is what makes REITs so attractive. They offer an option with a lower capital cost to enter what is known as the asset type. A drip is what many REITs offer. A drip can be described as a dividend plan. These plans can allow you to have access to commercial realty for as low as one stock share that can be bought. Additionally, there are very few fees. Nearly every mutual funds company has a

REIT focus option. Many mutual fund companies offer REIT-focused options. This means you could get started investments starting at $500, or even $2,500. This is a cheaper option than buying a house, or property to rent.

If you're looking for physical property and are ready to invest more, there are other options. Everybody should aim to acquire physical real property. Even if only one person is interested. It is possible to join a group of real estate investors or a private partnership. At the core, real estate investment organizations allow investors to own multiple units or one unit in what is known self-contained living spaces. This could be done in a condo or apartment building. Or through an operating business. If the company is operating, it manages all of the units and handles all aspects of maintenance including advertising. In return, they receive a percentage from the monthly rent.

Investors will be happy to find out that the investor still holds the property. They still own the property. This makes the realty group a cost-effective option for anyone looking to invest in real estate. Real estate investment partnerships often require an investment from $5,000 to $50,000. Although $5,000 isn't enough to purchase an average unit in a building, many partnerships exist to pull money from multiple investors.

This is known collectively as shared and crown by several investors. A real property investment group or partnership could give you a monthly income, but not as much as buying the property.

It is possible to purchase a property, or you can become a landlord. However, it is the most expensive way to invest in real estate. This is a very common idea. It is simple. You go out and purchase property. You rent out the property to tenants. The mortgage, maintenance tax and other charges are paid by the owner of the property. Rent should be charged at a reasonable amount to cover all costs. This will result in a loss of income and a decrease in your financial stability.

There is also a credit crunch. There is no concept of a "no document mortgage" anymore. It is gone. And it has been gone for years. Potential property owners will be required to provide at least 20% down payment by banks. The down payment must amount to 20% of the property price.

Imagine that you're buying a $100,000 home. This will show you just how costly it is. It means you must put down $20,000 because that is 20% on $100,000. However, they won't tell anyone that the $20,000 that was just spent didn't include closing costs. That could take $5,000 from your budget. It also doesn't contain any fines. Your total spending is $25,000 already.

It is important to check that everything is working properly before you buy a property. If it's not up-to-standard, tenants could be unhappy and it could even lead to a lawsuit. Many landlords have made the same mistake and have been heavily fined. Many others ended up in court as a result of their tenants getting extremely high settlements from negligent landlords. For example, if you buy a house constructed before 1978, your tenant must be given a pamphlet about lead and lead paint. The tenant could sue you and get a settlement. You must also be aware of issues such as foundation and mold, or any old foundation that might become unstable.

There are many factors that will make your property rentable. These are just some of the repairs you can make. There are many things you need to do before you can rent your apartment. It is possible to end up paying more than $20,000, even if you spend all of it. You might end up paying a lot more than you realize. These higher prices could result in a much greater expense than the average investor.

It may end up costing more than you can afford in the long term. This means that you can have a long term investment in real estate, whether you want to actually own it or you use REITs (real estate investment groups). There are many ways to start. However, this all depends on what you put into it. There are many methods to get in the business without spending too little. But there are also many other ways you could get involved.

It all depends on what you are willing put out there. This is why you might want to consider hiring a professional financial advisor. The information that financial advisers have in this field is invaluable and they may be experts in something you don't. A financial adviser may be the best way to make big financial decisions. You might even be able to speak with someone who is more familiar with finances than yourself. This would also be a good idea. This is why we also suggest that you should learn accounting before entering this field.

This chapter's tips will help to figure out how much you can spend and where. This knowledge will help you avoid falling prey to the same pitfalls as other investors in real estate. You now have the confidence to know that you don't necessarily have to spend hundreds and thousands of money unless you decide to do so, and that there is a way to go up. These are things that your competition might not know. While many people don't like admitting their ignorance, it is important to be willing to put in the work to learn. This is what we want. Because if you are ahead and know what others don't, you're going to make the money. You are better than them. This is exactly the thing you should desire.

Chapter 7: Your Real Estate Team

This chapter deals with your real-estate team. Most people believe that a team of real estate agents is the same thing as the people working in the office. But, that's not the truth. The following people make up a team in real estate.

1. A real estate agent

2. A property renovating company

3. A home stager

4. A team leader (to handle the listing)

5. A team member (to help buyers)

There are many others you could add to this team but these five people are the most important. These are the people who will make the most impact. The following is a typical list of team responsibilities.

1. Buyer's Representation. This represents the buyer's support.

2. Listings. These are the specialists and coordinators who promote and produce the listings.

3. Listing agents. This is where the CEO comes in.

4. Communications and Marketing. This means listing promotion, as well as advertising and design.

5. Support. This includes administration, operations, coordination of transactions, and management.

In certain cases, your team may include both a group brokers and a list with buyer's agents. For smaller cases, this could only be two agents with an administrative assistant. Agents who work together enjoy a more balanced work-life balance. This leads to a better business. They can then spend more time on what they enjoy and less on what they don't.

Recent studies and reports indicate that almost 40% of agents believe that the team they are part of can be of benefit to the industry. In addition, more agents think that it is important to join a team to get experience and leads, as well as to mentor early in their career.

There are many benefits associated with hiring a realty team. The main ones are the following.

1. Real estate teams are capable of dividing and conquering. Sometimes, they're able do this much better that individuals.

2. Real estate professionals are always ready to assist clients. They understand the importance to be at the client's disposal.

3. Real estate companies are good for collaborating.

4. Teamwork in the real estate industry is a great way to increase your skill. The best way to increase your skill set is to become a part of a team.

5. The problem of feeling alone in a real estate team can be avoided.

6. It is possible to have a better life and work with real estate teams. Because you don't have to do this all by yourself, you have more time with family.

7. Real estate agents have the lead coverage.

8. Real estate teams make a stable income.

9. Real estate teams know how to leverage.

10. Real estate agents are great at teaching and training other people.

11. Real estate groups are good for specialization.

12. Real estate teams can bring in more leads and generate more income.

13. It is possible to sell a business through the use of real estate teams.

On the flip side, there can be downsides when hiring a real-estate team. These are two of the most important.

1. The bad apples can do more damage to the team than good.

2. You are not able to do your work effectively alone.

We've already discussed the benefits. Let us now explain why you should use each one.

Dividing is conquering

Teams of real estate agents tend to have a mindset that is more production-oriented. This when one person performs the same task repeatedly. Each person can be considered a specialist. This is because of their experience and talent. This means that you will have a team consisting of experts. This team focuses their efforts on refining one step of the transaction process. This team could be a coordinator, who will bring attention to listing through outlets or go into your paperwork to make sure it's correct. You can think of your team in terms of a line within a business, where everyone is doing their own job. It's almost the exact same idea for a team. One person might do one thing, and the next may do their own. This is how they get along well with one another.

Wear many aprons if you're an agent. Your abilities in marketing and negotiation may make them exceptional, but their ability to do other tasks could make them mediocre. You will have all your requirements met with a group.

Always ready for anything:

Studies show that people should always be willing to help clients. That could include holding their hand and helping them through anything they may need. This is true across many companies and for many different teams. When you have a team, someone is always available to answer any questions and help the client.

Your team will support you when things get really bad. This will make sure you're not stressed out or overwhelmed.

Excellent synergy

This word is ridiculed in modern society. The word is often used in a jokey way by companies, but it's an important part of the world. This word is often used by real estate teams and it means that they have synergy. A great collaboration is achieved when people come together. This is what it's worth because it will allow your team work more efficiently than it currently does. It will also make it easier for any bad apples to realize that they can work with you. This will allow you to get more wisdom, creativity, as well as more contacts than they already possess. Access to expert knowledge and skill-sets is also a plus.

Individual agents can, however, sell a house more quickly than a group of people. In truth, this may be true in some instances. This is why it is up to you to decide whether or not to hire a group. Everything will depend on your preferences and personal style. Do not let someone convince you that you want to work as part of a team.

Enhancing skill improvement

Experience is key when you are a rookie agent. A team can help speed up your learning curve. For you to get more listings and other opportunities, good teams will be able provide you with a listing stock. You will be able create more leads online, as well as hold open houses. This will increase your ability to obtain more leads and help you learn more about negotiation, time management, and sales. Real application of these skills will make it easier to achieve this goal. It is difficult to learn for new agents. And if you don't have leads, it's even more difficult. It is best to practice and get sales opportunities to help you improve these skills.

Do not be lonely!

Working alone can make sales lonely. Agents work alone and have very little social interaction. They no longer work 9-5. Being part of a team can prevent you from feeling isolated. They can collaborate with other people to help realize their vision. The benefits of this type of work are that you can feel connected to others. If you don't find this appealing, that's fine too. Each person is unique, and it's okay to not be able work in a group. It's up to you and what suits your needs.

Enjoy a higher quality of your life

A team leader can improve your quality-of-life. With a team, other people can get the coverage and support they need. This gives them more time with family members or allows them to recharge their batteries. The leader plans the schedule and is aware that clients can be helped even if they aren't working. It's helpful to have a support team during vacation and school. Everyone knows that your children will need to be with you more during vacation and school breaks. This means that your children want to be with and for you.

Better lead coverage:

Selling agents have 24/7 access to all real estate information. The job of an agent is to be able to work at all times. Failure to obtain an online lead will result in a lower conversion rate. Don't waste your leads by being unresponsive to them. This is a fast way to lose clients and money. People want someone to listen and to them. If you and the team don't communicate with each other, it will be difficult for them to cooperate. The team can support you while you recharge. They can also manage coverage opportunities. They can lead coverage opportunities, whether you're a leader of a group or a member.

Generating a stable income

Feast or Famine is one of life's greatest challenges. This is true across many industries, but the main one that is relevant to financial earning in cases is food and drink. It is possible for agents to have great months and then make very little. This is due to market fluctuations as well income cycles. Agents will have more difficulty controlling spending, cash flow, savings, and other financial aspects due to income cycles. The result is that they spend too much on the months that they do well, and they have less income for the months they don't. With swings in income, having a group of professionals can help. A team of professionals can help you when your personal production is lower. This is where the concept of "if you're weak at something, a colleague could be stronger" applies. This can help when you aren't making as much as your goal. As a leader you can share in the company's success. The consistency of your income will increase if you have a strong sales team.

This is one benefit to working with a team, rather than working by yourself.

Leverage is a concept that teams can understand:

Teams have a clear understanding of what leverage is. Listings are the greatest form of leverage you have. It is possible to create leverage by securing a listing. All other agents on the team should have access. You want agents who are able bring buyers and offers. Together, you can do this.

Another great source of leverage is having a team that can work hard on the listings and finding buyers. This is called human lever. Strong leverage is achieved when a team leader has more leads they can work with and create. This will decrease expenses and allow for more sales. This leads to higher sales profits.

They can coach or train others.

A great advantage of any job is the ability to train and coach others. It's rewarding and gratifying to be able help people communicate and to learn from them. Many people don't have skills like you. It is a great opportunity to learn from others and to help make them stronger. It can be an incredibly rewarding experience. You can also teach others how to achieve the same thing you've done. This will allow them to reach their goals, or strengthen your team. This is one your best rewards as a leader.

The benefits associated with specialization

Business is all about doing what you're good at. This means that if one of your strengths is not recognized, you can find someone to take over. This is a fantastic tip. It means you have a group that is strong in the areas you aren't and a team which is strong in the areas they are. It's a good idea to make sure you have everything covered. If you're weak in any one area, other people can exploit that and take the property from you. This is why your team must be strong. You can make your team stronger by having different skills. If you're starting in business, you don't need people who don't understand what they're doing. This is especially true if you want to be a serial investor. If you are a novice, no one will put their money in you. It is important to learn how to do so. Working with sellers and buyers will yield better results. This will allow you to list your properties and then follow up. This will increase your cash flow and give you more property options.

Your income and leads can be increased:

When you have a team working together to generate leads, both you and your income will increase. If a group works together to generate leads online and offline, it will help to maintain a balance. In turn, the team will be able create more income through the efforts they have combined. Because you know where to look for them, you can help your team start investing and purchasing property. This makes it easier for you and the team to make more. Each member does a particular job. If they all do it well, revenue can be earned. As revenue increases, you can purchase more properties.

Selling your business more easily

Most agents are solely responsible for their clients' businesses. It is important to have a team that helps you build a system and strategy. This can then be used by other businesses. You can use a team to make your business sellable and move it beyond you.

Let's talk about the negative aspects and the possible consequences of working together as a team.

Bad apples

Study after study shows that teamwork is not without its challenges. While most have positive results, others say that people can act out in the face of confusion. The confusion can cause them distress and even work against them. They state that they don't enjoy certain issues faced by teams, like the ones below.

1. There is a dearth of personal service. It is important to provide personalized service.

2. There are issues with not knowing whom to contact.

3. Poor communication. Communication is key to a team working effectively.

4. There are already preconceived expectations regarding how team leaders will deal with each other. Studies show that team leaders can be difficult to work with if they aren't given enough information.

5. They don't like being bounced around among members of different teams. This is an excellent thing. When you are being thrown around from person to person, it is difficult to see the important information clearly or to identify who is the leader. This can lead to anger and confusion in some cases.

Solo working:

Some people love working alone. If you're looking for a way to develop a strong relationship with an agent one-on-one, a team may be not the best option. You can't go wrong with asking for help. But, it's fine to do things your own way. It's a decision you make. Some people may not have the necessary knowledge to run a successful business once they get started. They may have problems choosing a property to own or may need financing. These problems can be addressed by a team. People learn quickly and don't need one. There are many resources that you can use to learn. It's all about you.

Chapter 8: How To Map The Real Estate Search Area

The importance of mapping out the area for your real estate search is critical. If you can't navigate the property locations and determine which ones to purchase, you won't be able do anything. You must be able understand where you are needed to go and what path to take. Keep in mind that this market is highly competitive and you will need to be able win over others who are looking for the same properties.

There are many sources of mapping that you could use to locate real estate. Google

Maps and MapQuest are two options. Google Earth is another option. These sites will provide you with a listing of real estate map resources. Google maps is excellent because it maps the addresses of all US residents geographically, or by satellite. It can give you driving directions and even show you photos so that you can clearly see what you are getting. Google Earth offers a 3-D viewing service that you can use free of charge. You can also see the maps. If you want to map the real property area, it is best to be familiar with the area.

America has many excellent mapping sites. In order to accurately map real estate areas, it is essential to understand what kind of property your are searching for. If you're searching in the country, you won't find a Beverly Hills-style mansion. Knowing the address of your property is going be a great way to find out where you are looking. While you may be able to find property by knowing where it is located, you will need to know what you want.

We won't go into too many details as we've already talked about this in other chapters. Once you decide what type of property is important to you, you will know where to search. If you live near the property you want to view, you have two options. You can also use great mapping services or take a drive. BatchGeo can be a great tool for real estate. It lists all properties in the area, as well as sales. It also lets you map open houses. It has all the data you need. You can index the properties by their square footage, year of construction, taxes and even see photos. It allows you to view property addresses and lists agents. These maps make it easy to find what you are looking for. If you can do this you will be able better map out the realty area. You'll also be able locate properties that aren't visible to others.

BatchGeo's popularity is not limited to real estate professionals. This is because it is useful for anyone who is looking for property or is trying to enter this business. Because they allow you to list agents and brokers, and you can create maps to visualize both your brokerage listings and your regular listing in one place. All that is required is the address. You can visualize your listings to buyers agents, show you maps for sale, map houses for sale, and you and your clients have access to listings of maps all around the internet. If your goal is to buy a house, this will likely require a lot more research. It takes hard work, so you will probably have a spreadsheet listing potential properties.

Visualizing your work makes it easier. A batchGeo maps can help you to map the recent sales of comparable properties. Also, real estate data can be collected, which is a huge asset. There are many websites that provide real estate data. Agents and brokers are likely members of multiple listing platforms like we have mentioned. If you have access, and if your research is thorough enough, you may be able create your own spreadsheet. These sites are great at helping you find that information. BatchGeo requires only basic information. Once you have this data, you can create maps and search for the best properties.

Smart agents will embrace today's technology because it allows them to excel in a world of competition. Others might still be using brochures or using a Rolodex. But these outdated methods are no longer relevant in today's market. Although you can still use them and hope to be as successful in the future as you were in the past, it's not the right thing to do. The best thing is to embrace the future. Because it's constantly changing and growing, and you don't know how to adapt to its growth, you could be left behind.

Zillow is an example of this. Real estate technology has been booming. Zillow provides one of the best tools to search for properties and to map the area. You can choose the exact criteria you need to find exactly what your looking for. Another reason you should be able to identify what it is you are trying to rent, sell or buy.

The residential market's potential is great because the internet allows you to easily expand your listings and to search for exactly where you want to go. Keep your listings up-to-date. This will make it easier to map out real estate areas more accurately. Google Earth has changed the way we view data. We have all used google maps. Google maps is a revolution that has millions of users every day. The satellite imagery is one the most valuable data resources you can use from the internet.

You can see every home you'd like to buy and all of the areas that you want. A benefit of this is that you'll be able to see what areas are most profitable and which should be avoided. You also have land marketing specialists who can draw and market your land. Everybody wants easy tools to access property information. You can open up the map to see what you're looking at and then you can get the data. It also allows you to see the community and will allow you to access their parcel data.

You can use them as file or map services. There are layers upon layers which show you more than photos. You can view attributes and draw in the proper way if you want to remember what your house looks exactly later. Many people use this option to visualize what they want. They also support social networks and online sites, such as Flickr or Facebook. Facebook is huge. Some people don't even know the basics of Flickr. You should not dismiss it. You can still use the photos once they have been taken.

What mapping out the area of real estate means is, in a nutshell, that you use sites to look for rental properties. You also need to know how to best utilize the search bar and map buttons. The goal is to find the best properties in the region.

The map can also be used by a real estate agent because they have already scoured areas in search of a profitable property. However, the majority of people don't want them to be there if they are going it alone. You'll need to learn how search buttons work if you're trying to find property by yourself. This is particularly true if the goal is not to find a professional real estate agent.

You can search for information at most of the sites we have mentioned in this book. If you look at the top screen of the websites you use, you will see a button that says Search or a feature that states Search. Search by entering the address of your home or the desired area, and it will list all available rentals in that region. If you want to search for a certain price, then you can input the minimum and maximum. This will allow you to be in the financial area that you desire.

If you aren't interested in renting properties and want to buy one, all that's required is to switch from rent for sale to view all the properties available to you. This will give you a list of all the properties available to you for purchase or investment. Then, you can start to buy them.

If you're specifically looking for something like one or two bedrooms, you can narrow down your search to those criteria and make sure you are finding what you are looking. You can also refine the search results by adding bathroom options. You can choose to have one bathroom or 2 bathrooms. All the sites mentioned in this guide have search options that allow you find property. Some may differ from one another, but all of them have the same features that allow you to search for property. They are also great resources for people who want to map out the area.

These sites offer you the ability to select what you're specifically looking for. Many sites also allow you to enter additional features that will further limit your options. Will your home allow pets? Do you allow pets in your home? You can also search the internet for those items. For example, if you have a small pet or a large dog, you can search for those items. All these are options that you can input into your search engine to find a home, or property that's exactly what you want. Although you have the option to ask the seller if they will allow pets to live in their home, it is best to find out if your potential houses offer the same.

Being able and confidently navigate these sites will make you stand out from your competition. This will also enable you to find the properties that are right for you. This skill is essential to you and your company. Surprisingly, most people don't know how Facebook or Zillow works. This is why we emphasize the importance of technology. If you don't know what to do with it, you might be left behind and end up losing your property.

Understanding these features will enable you to ensure you're using these sites to its best advantage. Also, you'll be able better understand this industry than those who don't use the sites or have no knowledge.

Chapter 9: How To Select The Right Property For Rent

This is one the most important decisions you'll ever make. Which property are you going rent? Consider a variety of factors when you are making this decision. They are:

1. What is the best area for your property to be? This can be further broken down to city areas or rural areas. Do you want to live in a large urban area or in the countryside? Do you want close proximity

to landmarks or do you prefer to be a little more isolated from other people?

2. How are the schools around the area you are interested in (many people feel this doesn't matter). Even if they do not have children, this really matters and tells a lot of about the area.

3. What is your area's crime level (their tenants want to be in a safe area)? What is the risk of someone getting hurt in your area?

4. What is the exterior and interior look of the property?

5. Are you moving to a residential area or into a business area?

6. Which price point do you prefer?

7. What amenities do your property need? For example, do you need a washer or dryer? Do you need a microwave and a dishwasher? California is home to many apartments without any of the above. Many apartments lack the latter two but have a shared washer/dryer.

There are many other questions that you must ask yourself. These questions will help to clarify what you're looking for in a home and in the area. It is important to understand why this is important. For example, you might own the most beautiful home in the community, but it may not be in an area with high crime rates.

Many people will experience this when they first start their journey. You may find a lovely house and think it is perfect. But then, you start to see the mess that is going to consume every penny of your savings. You need to do your research and be thorough. Avoid mistakes so that you don't have them to make again. Because no one can be perfect, it is worth noting that mistakes are possible. We want to help minimize those mistakes and ensure that they don't cost too much. It's much easier than fixing costly mistakes.

There are many things you need consider in order to make an informed decision when buying a property. There are several things that you must be aware of, and you can also rely on your intuition and your common sense. Be sure to verify that the property is suitable for your needs. It is important to remember that property owners have many other responsibilities than you might realize. These include how to deal effectively with troubled people. What are your options if the lights go out or the roof is damaged? If forced to do so, would you be able and willing to get rid of people?

There are a few things you should ask yourself. Do you know how unclog a bathroom? Are you an electrical engineer? Do you have any construction experience? Are you at least familiar with the tools and how they are used? Cost and teams are the main reasons for this questioning. If you have to find someone to do this job for you or a team of people you will be reducing your profit.

On the other hand, most homeowners have at minimum one home that they can repair themselves. This helps to protect their profits. These questions are important because if you cannot fix anything in the property (e.g. foundation problems) then you might not want the property to be as expensive. If you must pay someone to fix it, you can ask for a better price. This also has its downsides. Depending on your specific circumstances, a house that is less expensive may not bring you any profits.

A common warning for real estate investors: if landlords aren't for you, it might be too difficult. This does not mean that property cannot be bought, but you will have less profit if someone else manages the properties. If this is your situation, you might find yourself a better person to help with crowd funding or taking classes to learn new skills. If none of those appeal to you, then it's time to hire a solid team of professionals.

Another thing to consider is that investors can choose to hold on to debt, but most investors don't want to. This is something to avoid, as it can cause greater harm than good. The reason is that most people have both medical bills and medical debt. This is in addition to the fact that many people have student loans. Depending on how far back you are, you may have children on their path to college. You will have to help these kids with their loans if it is not possible or what you wish for them. If you find yourself in this situation, carrying around debt will not be a wise decision. It'll also impact your ability choose the best property.

There is no reason to want to make it impossible to pay your debts in the real and the virtual worlds. This is where you need to be able to afford a safety margin. The higher interest rates will make it difficult to obtain a downpayment. Without that, you might not be able choose the property. It's not wise to buy a fixer upper property as your first.

It can be tempting to buy an inexpensive fixer-upper. You may believe that you can easily flip this house with the help of television. Some people are excited that they sell for less, and you might feel confident enough to try it. However, you need to have some knowledge in construction and electric and plumbing. Another reason is that you probably won't have someone to do it for you. Also, it can be quite expensive to find one. A team of professionals can cost a lot to clean and renovate a house. This is particularly true for quality work. You may find people willing to offer low prices for quality work, but these are very few.

All this means that the fixer-upper you bought for less than you paid will end up costing you at most twice what it cost and you may not even be able to make it sell for that price. Due to the amount of things we have in our lives and the needs of our families, we tend to be more economical. Times are difficult and getting more difficult, so we have no choice but to try our best. It's possible to lose your job. Remember that the market is volatile. Even those who invest a lot of money in property. Some people won't pay that much. And if you rent the home out, the rent might be too much because you are trying to recover your costs while making a profit. If you are looking for a home at a lower price, but with minor repairs, keep in mind the above questions. A house with minor repairs is going to be a lot cheaper than one with major repairs.

You should also remember that you might be able, if you find a property that is slightly cheaper on the marketplace and has minor repairs as opposed to something that costs more or has more serious repairs, that it will be possible to flip. Repairs can take up 6 months or more depending on what is wrong with the house. Minor repairs, like a roof leak, take about a week to fix. Roof leakage can be considered minor. However, serious problems may occur if the foundation is damaged or there's no insulation or it's electrical.

Problems such as these can be more difficult and you may have to wait until it is resolved. Your tenants cannot be moved into unsafe places. It's better for your tenants to move into a home that has minor repairs and is cheaper than one that is more expensive. They are much easier to fix than something more serious and take far less time. Leaking toilets can be much more expensive than flooding in the basement or a faulty AC unit.

It is also worth noting that many people tend to avoid moving into houses that need major repairs. You'll have solved the problem by time the tenant moves in. Your tenant may not be happy with the way it turned out, even though you did everything right. This is because they might fear that it will happen again. This is the reason why many people avoid older houses. People will avoid these houses as they are perceived to have issues and should be avoided. Others will avoid houses located in poor neighborhoods as they may be susceptible to the same problems. Allow them to walk through the house with you and tell them what it looks like.

The cost of a property will be another factor you should consider. Consider it this way: An operating expense for a new property is typically 30% to 75% of the gross operational income. Let's take an example: If you charge $1400 for rent, and your expenses are $500 per month, then your operating expenses will be 40%. You can also use the 50% rule to simplify the calculation. This means that if your rent is $3,000 per month, then your expenses (total expenditures) should be $1,000. Your return should be calculated as well. Ask yourself how much you will get back for every dollar you invest. It won't be worth it if you don't see a return for your dollars.

Now, we are able to really dive into the details. We are going to show you how important it is to find a low cost house. It is important to remember that the bigger your property or home, the more you will have to pay for your ongoing expenses. Experts in the industry recommend that you buy a home starting at $150,000. This may seem huge, but real estate is a lower market and the 20% downpayment would be $30,000. Although closing fees are still approximately $5,000 or $6,000, this would make it almost $40,000. However, this is still considered a lower level real estate.

Finding the right spot is important, too. It is important to keep this list in mind as you consider location. How dangerous is it? What are the schools like? A good area should have low property taxes, at minimum, a decent school system. But, it is important to aim for a quality school system and low crime rate, as well as an area with a growing labor market. The area should also be close to many amenities. The area should have places like parks, malls, or restraints. California is an example of such a place.

One mall is particularly located in a car park that surrounds it with restaurants and bookstores. To the east, north, and south there are houses and apartment blocks. They are desirable because they offer jobs in malls and stores, as well as being close to all the amenities. This knowledge will allow you to make wise decisions when it comes to your property. It's important to find out where people want live and why. Imagine the place you would choose to live. You wouldn't choose to live near crime. Why would your tenants want that? Your family doesn't want to be sent to a bad school. The same goes for your tenants. It will help you understand the mindset of your tenants or buyers by asking these questions. Look for areas with rising property values and young workers. For this, household growth is a huge advantage. Affordability, lifestyle, and availability of work are all important considerations.

Another tip is to be aware of the cities in which large companies are moving and those that have new headquarters. Amazon, for instance, made it clear last year that they were opening new headquarters. This led to the conclusion that people will be most comfortable in areas where they have their second headquarters.

Two-years ago, another study showed that companies are moving to urban areas more frequently. This includes metropolitan areas of bigger cities like Atlanta.

It is important to consider the difference between risk and reward. Your passive income can be a source of reward. Other than the initial investment and the cost of maintaining the property you will make, you can also earn money by putting your effort and time into your normal job. You don't just make rent. You should also increase your real estate investment as the value of real estate increases. Rental income is not subjected to social security tax. It can be put into a selfdirected IRA. Real estate is generally more stable than stock, which is why the tax savings on interest paid on an investment property are significant. These are just a few of the many reasons to consider renting the perfect home.

The potential risks of choosing the perfect property is also important. Although rental income is passive, it can be extremely difficult to manage without a property management agency. Even then, it can still be difficult. The adjusted gross income should be another consideration. If it exceeds $250,000 as a married couple filing jointly (or $200,000 as an individual), you may need to pay a surtax. This surtax does not include rental income.

Real estate can't be sold as quickly as stocks. You can't also sell a property piece-by-piece. It's not possible to sell a property piece by piece. Real estate costs are prohibitively high. Without a tenant, you'll be paying all expenses. You may not have enough rental income to cover the mortgage payment.

One of the most important things to do when looking for a great property is to be realistic. Renting isn't going to make you rich. It won't. At least it won't for a while. You could be in serious trouble if you pick the wrong property. You might also need to rent your home out to get a better idea of how you can be as a landlord.

The age of a property, or house you're considering purchasing, is not necessarily a good sign. In particular a real estate income property. It is mandatory that you show potential tenants or tenants any house built before 1978.

An older home should not be feared. The purpose of this article is to tell you that older properties might need more tender loving and care as they age than newer ones. It might have problems in the foundation or the insulation. These are just a few of many problems. Because older homes have been around for so many years, they tend to have more issues than their younger counterparts. It is important to look at the age of the income property relative to the other homes in this area.

A step back is a good thing if you're looking to purchase the newest house on the block. The old saying, "You should buy the worst home on the best street" is something you should keep in your mind. Remember, when it comes to selling the property you bought, it will be much more difficult to move the priciest house down the street than the cheaper one. You might purchase out of the state in an unrecognized area. Additionally, you need to get to know the neighborhood and not just the city. This is especially important when you are considering moving out of state.

This is why you will find information in many places that are suitable for finding property. This applies even if your ability to go there is limited. The appeal of different areas should help you determine your desired outcome. However, the success of evaluating appeal depends on your investment style. The homes in the most desirable neighborhoods are likely to be more costly but come with lower risk. This situation might bring lower yields but could provide more stability. However, lower-rated communities can yield higher yields. But, renter instability often means that they have less cashflow. You won't be paid if your renters don't want to pay the rent. When you start to put together your investing strategy, you should consider how comfortable with risk and return. It is important to calculate your return investment on every dollar that you invest. You must know what you're getting in return.

Renting is another important aspect to consider when looking for the best property. The final thing you should consider is whether the market is stable or growing in rental demand. You should avoid putting cash in areas where it won't give you anything. You want to have steady cash flow, and not intermittent.

There are many things to consider when assessing rental demand for real estate. First is population growth. This is easy to verify because all you need to do is log in to the US census bureau and search for growth trends by area or state. Because this will give a sense of how in-demand the property is, you should also look at how long it has been listed. Zillow can be a great resource for this information. Zillow offers a significant advantage over other real estate websites or apps. It's been around quite a while now, and has become a favourite among many. It will also tell you how long it has been on that site. If it hasn't been on the site in 6 months, then it means that there isn't much demand. It was more popular if it had been there for just 3 days before being picked up. It's possible to see what people desire by looking at the differences.

Also, make sure to check out the number and availability of rentals compared to the listed listings. To make this task easier, you can do some spying. You only need to call a manager and ask them questions about the rental market in the area where you are looking. Knowing your target tenant will also help you find the best investment property. If you're looking for investment property, ask yourself: "Would this property appeal to my tenants?" If your gut or common sense are telling you otherwise, this is probably not the right property for you. The vacancy rates are another important aspect to consider. The vacancy rates represent a percentage (or number) of vacant units from the total inventory available in any given area. You can also access the US Census bureau's website to see the vacancy and home ownership statistics by state and MSA.

It doesn't matter how well you know your landlord, it can make a big difference in helping or hurting them. Have you ever heard the expression, "Give the people their wants"? This will be true. It is essential to find out what people want in order to select the best property. Everyone's heard about millennials. All the talk about millennials is about how they are ruining everything. However, they can provide excellent information on what kind of property you should rent. Remember that millennials will be the future, and you should not ignore them.

Our first example will prove useful to college students and millennials. If you wish to rent your property out to college students, millennials, or other groups, you need to have a broad view of their needs. Students and millennials love nightlife. After a long study day, they want something to do. They also want to be in close proximity to career centers, as they are trying for a job. They also want to be close transportation since they have to travel back and forward and many don't own a vehicle. Because most college students have limited resources, and most millennials do not have enough money to buy a home, affordable housing is the most important thing they desire. They may be eligible for financial assistance from their parents, which is possible with the help of many. To help themselves get to school, work. This group may be worth renting if they can afford lower rent.

If you have baby boomers, they'll want to be close to healthy options. The property should be in close proximity to shopping centers and grocery stores. These are places they also like to be near, such as fitness and recreation centres. They want their happiness to be there. Nature-loving baby boomers like the rest of us, enjoy walking trails or places in the natural world. They want to live in areas where they are able to exercise and enjoy a healthy lifestyle.

If you own a single household home, then you will get the singlefamily renter. The single family renters might be someone who is moving from their parents' place to the marital home or a couple who has been married for awhile. Even someone who is just looking to live in their own home. Single family renters want a yard for their pets, or for their children, if they have any. If they have children, it is likely that they want the good school district that we mentioned earlier.

Many of them want privacy because they don't want their neighbors knocking at the door every five mins. Rental properties can appeal to families with children. Families like to do things together, such as spending quality time with their kids. This knowledge can be used to you advantage. Families enjoy activities that are family-friendly, such as going to a zoo with their kids, swimming lessons at a pool for their children, or books and movies for the whole family.

You will be able to think about your tenants differently if you do this. Realize what your tenants want and you can give it to them. This will help you be a better landlord. If you apply all of the tips and tricks that we have provided in this chapter, you'll be able select the best property. This chapter will help you choose the best property that suits your investment needs. You need to keep in mind that your financial situation and portfolio will be affected by the choice of the best property. You may not be able sell the property if everything is done correctly.

The best salespeople have a clear understanding of what their clients are looking for and know how to deliver it. This is a good tip for real-estate because renters will stick with you if they get what they need. They will also recommend you to others if your renters leave. This will increase cash flow and make sure you have a steady income. When this happens, you can rent more properties and invest in more. Once you're more experienced, you should be able to identify market trends as well as the investment style you prefer. This will help you be able to buy better properties in future.

Chapter 10: How To Manage Your Rental Properties

When you rent out properties, it is important to understand how to manage them. If you don't properly manage your properties, you will quickly find yourself in trouble. Another reason to have a team is to help you. This is not a bad thing. It's okay to need help. Having a team can help you make it more manageable.

There are two ways to manage your properties. You have the option of either hiring a property manager, or self-management. These tips are key to managing your rental properties in a professional manner. You should realize that this is not as simple as it seems. Be aware that it is necessary to establish the market rent in order to rent property. Also, this will help you to estimate the cost of a house to rent. This will let you know if this is a good investment. You should realize that rental properties are a great investment but can be difficult to manage. Some individuals can manage 20 properties or more on their own; others require a team.

While multifamily houses are easier to manage than single family homes, managing commercial properties can be more difficult. You must be firm with your tenants and pay attention your details. You can't overlook the problems. You can't ignore the issues, and a good investment will be a bad one.

Make sure you compare different rental rates. It is not a good idea to choose the highest rental rate and assume that you will get the same rent. Most people choose to go with the lower-priced options, but you should be wary of scammers on sites such craigslist. If you're looking at Zillow or Craigslist and see a house you like, don't hesitate to post it. This will tell you which houses have been rented. You could call the properties to further explore this option. This will allow you to decide the price you should charge for your rentals.

You have the option of pricing high and hoping for renters to pay higher than the market, or you could price lower and find great renters.

Many people will use Zillow and Facebook to advertise your rentals. Trulia, another app, is also an option. Some agents may not recommend posting it on multiple listings, but others think it's helpful. This will be your decision when advertising your properties. Some say they rely heavily upon multiple listing sites in addition to other methods of advertising their rentals. It's important that you do your research on the most effective ways to promote rentals in your community. This will help to decide the right tool for you.

There are many places to place your listings.

1. If you have one, consider creating your own website. If you do have one, ensure you are using SEO practices in order to rank higher in search engines. SEO writing is the art of using keywords in search engines to help them rank higher. If you don't know what it means, the easiest way to explain it is to use the following definition: This is because you will be more visible on the list. Another tip is that your site should be optimized for mobile. This is an extremely important tip. It has been shown that 50% of mobile users will abandon your website if it takes over 3 or 4 seconds to load. Some users will wait only 2 seconds. People these days want instant gratification. If they don't receive it, they will move onto the next thing.

2. Craigslist. Craigslist used to be a frightening place but by using good judgment and managing it properly, it's now easy to navigate. It's a cheap place to post listings. Unfortunately, you will get lots of inquiries and emails. Some aren't serious. Craigslist is sometimes considered dangerous because of the number of people who have died responding to ads. A movie was also made about it. So it's wise not to be too cautious with your information and to use commonsense. It is also a good idea that someone is with you to protect you.

3. Realtor.com. Realtor.com is a website that handles both real estate sales, and rentals. They only accept listings that are owned or managed by property managers. Although their interface is not as attractive as Zillow's, it offers a simple search function that allows you to locate and price your property. Many people prefer this site as it's been around since a while and has been used by many.

4. Zillow. Zillow, one of the most popular websites on this list, is also very attractive. Their interactive map makes it easy to navigate. It also allows you to sort your search by specific features, such as price, bathrooms and pets. It's not limited to property rentals. There are many ways to search, including for properties that are for sale. This search tool can be used by both older and younger generations. This system is easy to use, regardless of how technologically proficient you are. You can also view listings from street view and have the option to upload photos. It also allows you to compare the listings.

5. Trulila. Trulia is very similar to Zillow. It has the same features as Zillow. The maps are slightly different. And you see the posts in slightly different ways. It is still highly effective and preferred by most users to other sites. It's easy to use and offers valid information.

6. Rentalhouses.com. Although it is a little older than other sites and a bit outdated, this site allows owners and managers

access to a nationwide rental database. Some people prefer it because it's been there for a while. They believe it may have some benefits that others don't.

7. Zumper. Zumper, which is also known as value added, is a website that offers what is called. It's still relatively new. Many people love it because of its innovative technology. Zumper provides city and neighborhood information guides, which tenants enjoy because it is not available on other sites. It allows you to upload one image for your initial listing. It also allows you to provide detailed listings so you can add a paragraph on the property. People value details. They don't want to see a simple picture of the property, with no details. Be sure to include all details and to convince the viewer that they should buy or rent your property.

8. Social media. Social media is used every day by everyone and it's one platform that you can use for your own benefit. Don't underestimate non-housing web sites as a way to market your rental property

listings. You can also advertise to your community via social media if you have a listing either on your website or on a site. Another advantage to social media is its ability to help you reach beyond your local community to reach people across the globe. You can also connect to people from all over the world. You could also create a social media listing with the details of your property in case you have trouble renting that property. Though they may not be property specific, Instagram, Twitter, and Facebook let you reach people and make it more community-like. They allow you reach millions of people each day and let them appeal to thousands. This allows anyone who moves across the country to see your property and can either rent or buy it. Facebook appeals to people older than others, so this works well. It appeals equally to all classes. Facebook is popular among the wealthy as well as those with less money. Both classes have to live somewhere so Facebook should be used for listings.

9. Airbnb is an online rental site that connects homeowners directly with short-term tenants. Airbnb has been a prominent player in home rental sharing over the past few years. They are also very dominant in peer to peer sharing or accessing services and goods. It is popular with many different age groups, including college students as well as millennials. Travelers love this site, but so do people who want to experience new things. You can also stay for several weeks, if you so choose. This can make vacationers feel happy as they don't have spend as much.

10. Apartments.com might be a little more old than others, but it still offers great benefits. They provide excellent care and offer good deals. Users can also save money upfront if they rent through this site. It's also free to everyone. Many people don't love the idea of owning a house. Others prefer apartment living. A second thing to consider is that most people who move from their parents house to their own property start with

apartments, and not houses. Apartments are usually cheaper than houses. Additionally, many people share their apartment with roommates. An apartment might work better for them.

11. Facebook. Facebook has over 500,000,000 users who use the group every day. They have groups for almost everything. Property falls under this category. The site also offers a highly customizable function to search for locations. It offers the possibility to increase the search radius by miles. This is an excellent way to make your contacts on Facebook aware of your rental properties. You can also use this to increase your income and generate more revenue. Many people follow these groups and have hundreds of members, which means they will see your listings. This gives you an advantage over your competitors and allows you to be seen by others who use the social media platforms. It is possible to outperform the competition by using them and not them.

The properties will need to be repaired and your prices set. As we discussed before, it is also necessary to be able maintain the properties after you rent them out. You'll need to collect rent from tenants as well as know how you can evict. This is vital because it happens and you have to be prepared. Accounting is another topic you will need. You will need to be able to perform it quickly if you aren't already.

A list of tenant requirements is a must when you're worried about tenants. The following items are included in the list.

1. Employer requirements

2. Credit score should not be below a certain level

3. Minimum income

4. Do you really want people to smoke? While you might be okay with this, smoke can cause damage to furniture. If it happens, you will be the landlord responsible for fixing it.

5. Do they require references (many people ask for them because they want to be sure that the person is trustworthy and reliable)? They also want references to determine if they can rent well.

6. Do they need their rental history to prove their income (most of them, if you don't need it all the time)?

After you've rented the property out and have posted your ad, it's time to find good tenants. They will respect you, and pay on the due date. That's all you need. You must find people who will not cause unneeded problems. This is very important and it could prove to be crucial during the rental process.

You should carefully read the contracts you have already written and make sure they are well-written. This is another tip that will help manage your properties efficiently and make it easier to do this with ease. Discuss the rental agreement thoroughly with the tenant. You will both be able to help the tenant and answer any questions they may have.

This will ensure that there are no misunderstandings and that everything is clear. To ensure they see the property, it is important to do a final walk-through together. As many details about your property as possible should be documented and photos should be taken. This way, if anything happens, you have proof of the property and can defend yourself in the event it happens. You'll also need to ensure that the tenant stays in their property. You can fix any problems with the fire alarm, air conditioner unit or other property-related issues as the landlord. You have to ensure that everything runs smoothly and that they feel safe.

Some landlords choose to do walkthroughs just once or twice each year. Others do it more frequently. It keeps communication open between you, your tenants, as well as ensuring that you are 100% satisfied with the condition of your property. Tenants have a tendency to damage property. This is a problem that all landlords recognize and deal with regularly. This could lead to serious property damage if you choose your tenants incorrectly. This is something landlords want to avoid because it has cost them their finances. Tenants that know you are coming will be less likely make damage because they will be more concerned about your thoughts.

You'll need a reliable list of contractors to ensure regular maintenance of your property. Local landlords might be willing to assist you so make sure to include them in your list. It is possible to fix basic issues yourself, so you won't need to hire someone. The best toolboxes are useful and every landlord should ensure they have basic tools to repair the property.

Above all, it is essential that you have a special maintenance fund. It should be used for any issues and maintenance that you may need. This is essential. This is crucial. If you need to borrow money to fix your home, then you're not only losing any money, but you're also making it worse. This is exactly what you don't want. You should also have regular checks on appliances like AC units, water heaters, or anything else of this nature. These appliances can be expensive to repair. It is possible for a water heater to burst and cause flooding. This is an additional expense. You should make sure that your heater is operating properly and doesn't require repair. The panel on the wall that regulates the temperature is susceptible to damage. A short circuit could also cause an electrical emergency. This is something else to monitor. The fire alarms must always be functioning in the house. You as a landlord should ensure that they are connected, as it is illegal for them to be disconnected in your home. You as the landlord are responsible for the inspection of the home by a fire marshal and police.

If it is a large repair you will have to hire someone. You have to ensure that they have housing in the event of a major incident. It can take some time, so it is important to understand that they may need your help to find alternative housing. This is especially true in cases where the repairs take several months or more. Sometimes, repairs can cause families to be displaced from their home.

Naturally, you'll need to ensure you collect your rent. Each landlord has his or her preferred method. Some landlords prefer checks and others money orders. However, there are those who prefer electronic collection. There are pros and con to each method so you can decide which one you prefer. You can see that checks can sometimes get lost and take some time to process. Your bank may bounce the money or move it. When you finally realize you don't need enough, you can pay your rent. It can happen to electronic services, too. In some instances, they charge fees every time you are charged rent. Renters may pay $20 each month to use electronic services. The additional $240 in fees per year means your tenants are paying an extra $240. This is something many people don't realise and it can cause them great distress.

You can't force them to pay if you raise the rent. This must be communicated to your tenants so that they can adjust. You also need to have a policy concerning late fees. Your tenants should be aware of it as it will impact you both. This is a crucial issue in managing properties. Many tenants have taken their landlords in court for raising rent, and they have been forced to pay. This is something you should be aware about before you rent out your home.

You may have to evict tenants. This can create problems. It is not something tenants like to do. The first thing you need to do is to give them an official notice. This should include details about how long they have until they fix the problem, and how long your property has to be left. If they fail to comply with the notice terms, you'll need to file an Eviction Notice with the

Court. It is possible to nullify an eviction order if you accept payment during the process. The eviction process can be complicated. Make sure you know your local laws. Although it may sound extreme this can help you avoid future financial hardships. Do not let the situation become one where the tenant knows more than you about the law. It is important that you wait for the court order and the local sheriff, to actually evict the tenant. This is especially true when the tenant refuses leave.

Accounting is a major part of managing your properties. We recommend that you learn this skill as it is essential. There are classes to make this process easier. And taxes are something that you will need a good understanding of. If you don't understand accounting, it is best to find an accountant who does. This is a great tip.

Keep an eye out for changes as they occur. Some property managers may not have the necessary knowledge to handle all of the tax and accounting information. This is why you need to work with a team, or your own accountants. This is where a team may be useful. If the stress is too much, your team can help.

The property management company can provide information and reports that you need. Doing it by yourself can prove more difficult. A professional accountant is a good choice to help make this easier. Keep track of all your property upkeep and maintenance expenses. These are tax deductible. To make sure that your personal finances aren't mixed up with business finances, you should set up a bank account specifically for your business expenses. Also, you should set aside money for taxes and other fees that may be unexpected.

If you're a great property manager, you'll be able either to manage the properties yourself or in a team. A few basic skills are required to manage property. You will need to be capable of buying and repairing the property, setting up rent costs and requirements for tenants and finding tenants to rent the home. If you want to have cash flow and profits, make sure that the property is maintained and collected rent.

Manage your properties well and don't be afraid to ask for help. Make sure you're ready to go if your house needs repair. To ensure that your home looks its best, it's important to get it fixed before you begin taking photos. You want it to look professional and homey. People love to see the beauty in our homes so it is important that you take great pictures. It is important to ensure that your furniture does not have any tears, stains or rips. Also, make sure that everything is as neatly as possible in order to draw customers into the room. This will encourage them to rent from the property. Your property will look its best, and you'll be able rented out more properties. This will lead to increased cash flow for your business and more rental properties. This will allow you to stay ahead of the curve and help you succeed in the real-estate industry.

Chapter 11: How You Can Become A Serial Investor

As we mentioned in previous chapters it is very simple to understand more about a topic if you are familiar with its meaning. To sum it, a serial entrepreneur is one who invests with people who are not only able to coach but also have ideas and plans that are strong in a specific industry. They make sure their investors have previous experience in the particular industry.

In this chapter, we'll be discussing how to locate capital investors. This will allow you to see how serial investors should make relationships with bankers and their families.

Anyone can become your capital investor in this sector. A bank could invest in you, your relatives or even your friends. It is important to find the right investors. With the right investors you will be able rent out more houses as well as purchase additional homes. First, you need to learn more about the subject. You will learn more about what you should do in this area if your eyes are open to the right information. A serial investor must have a good understanding of the market prices and market trends. Additionally, you need to be able to finance and repair the properties as you manage them once you've acquired them.

The next step is to choose what it is that you wish to do. YouTube channels offer valuable information that can help investors learn to invest. You have options. You might choose to flip property or you might decide to wait. Every person is unique, so it's your choice. Whatever you choose, you need a tactic. Many people believe that being generalist is better than being expert. However, a specialist does not necessarily mean you are an expert. This is what will convince people to trust and invest in you or let you invest.

Find out where the cash is. Finding the money can be a difficult task. Banks typically require 20% down to rent a property. This means that for a $100,000 property you must put down $20,000. This is a significant problem for most people. There are still ways to reduce your down payment. Include options like purchasing as an owner occupant. It is important to note that the downpayment does not include closing costs and the cost associated with fixing up the property.

Do not stay in the learning phase. This will make it difficult to take action. Many people become so obsessed with learning everything that they fail to take action. This industry is complex and it's essential that you have the knowledge to succeed. You don't need all the knowledge, but you do need to be able and willing to invest in your property.

While you're learning, you don't have to purchase a property immediately. However, you can start talking to agents and lenders as well as learn more about potential details. This will assist you when you are ready to start investing.

One of the best ways to invest in serially in the realty sector is to flip houses or rent out rental properties. There are many ways to invest even in the home you already own. The house you own can be sold. It has been shown that homeowners who had lived in the home for a while can sell it at a foreclosure. And, guess what? Because they owned it, they made a tax-free profit. This is because they invested with the residence. This can make it possible to buy a property quickly and with minimal money down. You may also be able buy more than one.

This will ensure that you receive a great deal. This is key for becoming a serial investor. This is a way to save money and avoid potential dangers associated with real-estate investing. While you may think the main thing is flipping the house, it isn't. It is important to find the best deal. The great deal will increase your cash flow. This means that you will make more money each month. You can also build equity. This means you can take care of it even if there is a market crash. If you are unable to sell, you can always make a profit.

Increased cash flow means you can refinance property to borrow most of the money that you invested, then put it back in the market. The banks and lenders will offer you more money on future and current properties when you are able to get great deals. This is how serial investmentists make their income. Remember that serial investors are people who have good relationships with others. You must earn trust before you can establish a relationship. Then, you will make more. Many people agree with the idea that it is best to purchase rentals when you first start out.

If the property is less than its market value and you have great cashflow, it is a good investment. If you require assistance, you can hire a manager to assist with managing the property. They will be able help you make a more hands-off purchase. It is a good idea to look at single family homes first before you consider becoming a serial investment investor. You will be able to find incredible deals on these properties and your cash flow will be phenomenal with these properties.

Also, you might be able to find deals on investment properties. You can search multiple listing websites for them. Multiple listing services are another great way to find homes in your price range. Many people feel that this is an inefficient way to make a start as a serial investor.

However, there are many brokers and real-estate agents that say you do require a good broker to get these properties. Zillow is a great example of how to quickly get great deals.

As an owner occupant you will have an edge over other investors. Banks, such as Wells Fargo and property managers, often prefer owner occupiers to make the purchase. If you are looking for houses that are not on the market, there are many options. These properties can offer you great deals and are popular with both buyers and sellers. After making the property perfect, they fix any problems and then they start to sell it for more profit. Be aware that you want other people to lend your money when you become a serial investment investor.

For this to happen, you must ensure that your cash flow is sufficient and that you have enough equity to attract people who are willing to put their trust in you and make a return on their investment. You could also try to find sales from the owner.

This means that the sellers have not hired a realty agent to sell their home. This can provide you with great equity. This is due to the fact that most people who are selling their house themselves will be willing to negotiate a little more on the price.

Another great place to look for great deals and help you become an investor is auction houses or wholesalers. You should also consider these places because wholesaling could be another way to become a successful serial investor. It is a great method to get your foot into the door. However it takes more time and work. These techniques are used by most wholesalers to obtain contracts. Once you've obtained those contracts or done a double close, the wholesalers are able to make a profit. You should remember that many people are also looking in the same places as yours. Wholesalers can be a good place for investors to begin looking for deals. If they are able to get a great deal on the property and get it under contract, they will then simply sell it to another investor. This is great for most people who are just starting out. It's also very competitive. Many wholesalers offer a variety of deals that are easier to buy.

This knowledge can be used for investing in real estate. You will find that it is not easy but worth the effort. As long as you own the rental properties and have the cash flow, you can make a successful serial investor.

Chapter 12: Why Should An Investor Look At Real Estate As An Investment?

Real Estate as a Source for Positive Real Returns

Selection of the right asset classes and composition of an investment portfolio depends on many factors. Sometimes, an asset class is the reason. Sometimes prior knowledge or professional experience could be important. Sometimes it all boils down to availability. This aspect of real estate investing is often what seems to make it difficult to invest in this area. Why? The main reason is the way we think about real property. The vast majority of people believe that real-estate investing involves buying a property for at least five to seven figures. Nowadays there are many alternatives to purchasing investment properties outright. These alternative investment options require less capital. This has helped to reduce the minimum investment amount. A crowdfunding platform allows one to invest in realty. It lets you lend money to the property developer, acquire a small ownership stake, finance the purchase with large amounts of borrowing, or buy units in different realty investment trusts. We can all agree that real estate investment as an asset type is easier than ever.

However, you have a reason to choose asset classes for your portfolio. This isn't about the ease of access and investing. Your investment objective will be the main factor determining your investment portfolio composition. What is the ultimate goal of your investment venture? Why are you investing? What do you want to achieve by investing? No, this is not about promoting popular phrases like financial freedom or passive investments that generate income. No. These questions do not concern you. It involves the assets themselves.

Capital is required to invest. This is also known as savings. It is common to earn income by exchanging your time for cash. Employer, contractor, or entrepreneur. After spending a certain portion of your income, you can save the rest. These savings are our wealth. Our wealth. The first questions are about your wealth and assets.

What is your investment purpose? The following questions should be answered clearly. Would you like your wealth to be preserved? Or would it be more beneficial to you? Or, perhaps you want to preserve the purchasing strength of your wealth. Are you able to see the difference between these options? Let's take, for instance, the assumption that your savings would be sufficient to cover 12 months worth of living expenses such as mortgage or rent, groceries and transportation costs. The situation in which you could cover your 12 monthly living expenses within 5 years or 10 years is the latter of the three questions. What does this all mean in the context of investing? It simply means that when you want to preserve the purchasing ability of your savings or wealth, you should invest in asset types that have demonstrated to generate returns that are at least the same as the average inflation. This means that the average inflation rate (average increase in consumer prices) should be below 10%.

You should also ask one additional question when setting investment goals. Option four is growing your investment's purchasing power. This means that you should invest in asset types that are inflation-beating. To clarify, inflation refers simply to the annual rise in consumer prices. This figure is typically calculated in every country by the national statistic offices. These calculations use an average consumer basket as the base. This includes everything including milk and bread, medical care, education, transport, and other costs. What does this mean if we are to see an inflation figure of +5% This simply means that in the last year, prices have increased by an average +5% for all products and services.

That's right! While this may seem obvious, does future inflation not remain unknown? Isn't the future inflation, no matter how far out it goes, unknowable? This is true. It is possible to forecast the future expected inflation numbers. Professional economists can also forecast the future. However, future inflation numbers are generally unknown. As we get further into the future, the less certain we are about these forecasts. Your next question is likely already asking you: How can I make sure that my investments have the potential to outperform inflation in the future? How do I choose asset types that can provide inflation-beating yields for the future? This is easier than you may think. This is where history can help.

Empirical analysis of historical financial data shows that certain asset classes consistently provide inflation-beating total rewards. It is also known as positive real results in academic lingo. When discussing returns of financial assets, we often refer to nominal return. When we subtract inflation from the return figure then we are now referring to real returns. In other words, the real return is the sum of all returns from a financial asset and minus inflation.

To historical returns. As stated, some asset types have proven to produce positive real return over decades and decades. It might not be true in every calendar year. However, when we examine return numbers for long-term investing, the pattern is clear. What is the long-term? A long-term investment horizon of 10+ year is generally considered long-term. The following holds true for most cases, even when measured within a 5-year window. However, for both empirical and academic research, a 10-year perspective is the most useful.

So what asset classes have produced inflation-beating total results? Remember, real returns include the inflation rate. Thus, it is not uncommon for above-average inflation to be accompanied by double-digit inflation. For the United

States, this was also true in the years 1979-1982. Inflation for the US averaged nearly +10% during these four years (+9.6% to be precise). That's quite a lot. This is especially so when we compare it with the relatively low inflation figures for the past 10 year that we have become accustomed to. These +10% annual median inflation rate numbers are indicative that financial assets needed to earn positive real returns greater than +10% per year.

Let's examine some data. S&P 500 Stock Market Index, which tracks price movements from 500 US companies, produced the following returns for the four years in interest: +12.3% in 1979 and +25.8% respectively in 1980. These four years give us an average annual return in excess of 10,0%. The FTSE All EquityREITs index, which consists of US real estate investment trusts listed on the NYSE, showed the following return figures in these four years: +35.9%, +24.4%, +6,0%, +21.6%, and +35.9% for 1979. This amounts to an average annual yield of +21.5% for the period 1979-1982.

In order to obtain real return figures, subtract the average annual inflation rate from nominal return figures. We get the following results: US large capitalization stocks delivered an average annual positive actual return of +0.4% during the period 1979-1982. On the other hand, listed real estate returned an average of +11,9% above inflation. Isn't that a huge difference? This is just an example. It was only taken over a period of a few years. So there's no need to draw too many conclusions right now.

This graph displays the annual nominal yield data for US equities represented as S&P 500 and US-listed realty investments trusts represented as FTSE NAREIT All Equity REITs.

Figure 1.

In terms of returns, we can see there have also been poor years, average years, and great years. Over this 48 year span, the average annual US stock returns has been +7.8%. The average annual return on the listed realty investment trusts has been +11,000. Over the same period, the US experienced an average annual inflation rate of +4,0%. US stocks gave a positive real returns of +3,8% an annum, and listed real property +7.8% an annum above inflation.

Even though it may be easy to believe that listed real property investment trusts are more profitable than stock market returns now, it is far too early to discount stock investing. First, I want to remind you that the above analysis uses S&P 500 index stock market index as a proxy of equity market. This means that calculations above included only large capitalization stock. Small and medium-sized companies were not included in the calculations. Based on the history and performance of financial markets, small-cap stocks tend to have higher returns than large ones. The above analysis also focused on US markets. We need to take into consideration the data from other countries to make reasonable conclusions.

The following chart illustrates this. The data come from 16 developed countries. It considers the average annual real income (nominal returns minus inflation) of residential realty (physical realty) and stock exchanges. The panel on either side shows results for the period 1870 to 2015 (145 years), and the panel on both sides covers 65-years of data or the time period 1950 through 2015. The bars are the average real gains of different asset classes during the chosen period.

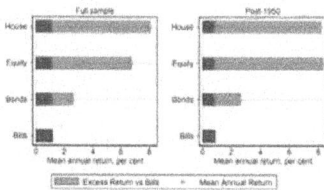

Figure 2.

This research paper and similar analysis can help us to conclude that the stock markets have historically returned around 6-8% annually. The average annual real return for investors in real estate investments has been 7-8%, depending on the form.

These two asset categories are best suited to growing wealth at an inflation rate higher than the average. There is one other thing we should remember. For real estate investments, the return figures take into account that a significant portion of the property's purchase price was financed through borrowed funds. The typical investor's personal funds only account for 20-25%. As a reminder, 75 to 80% of the property purchase price comes in the form a loan. Further, the above-mentioned return calculations assume that the property will be rented out and is earning rental income.

Therefore, real estate investments can be described as property partially financed with borrowed money and then rented out. These historical returns figures do not reflect the price appreciation of real estate. While price appreciation is an important part of the total result, rental income and the financial leverage used by real estate investors make up a large portion. Rent income has historically accounted for around half of the total real estate investment return, while price appreciation accounts for the other half.

If we look at investment funds that buy real estate objects or real estate investment trusts outright, the financial leverage comes from these trust and fund structure. This means that when a fund manager acquires a property, it will often be partially funded with borrowed funds. The average amount of borrowing by real estate firms, investment funds, and trusts is at least 50% of a property's purchase cost.

If your ultimate investment goal is growth of wealth and assets at a faster rate than inflation, stocks and realty are the best options. Specifically, it's possible to invest in rental properties and financial leverage.

Advantages & Disadvantages Real Estate as an Asset Type

The asset class real estate can be very emotional and can cause strong feelings. There are people who won't hear anything about how to invest in physical property, such as buying a rental property. People who don't want to hear about investing in physical real estate (i.e., acquiring rental properties) are likely to think about the obligations of tenants that don't pay rent on the due date or not paying it at all. Other people believe that real property is one of best asset classes. This is because you can physically see and touch the property, it is easy to manage, it's possible to make higher returns with good interior design, and most importantly, it has the potential to be leveraged financially to get high rates on your capital investment.

There is more. Low liquidity is a major drawback of real estate investing, according to investors who prefer financial investments. You can sell stocks from your investment portfolio in seconds. Selling a property might take weeks, if not months. Private investors might be at disadvantage due to the stock markets' high liquidity. Research has shown that the greater the total return stock investors receive, the longer they keep stocks (which means less trading) it is. It is possible to argue that the low liquidity associated with real estate properties can be an advantage. When selling is a time-consuming and laborious process, investors tend be more analytical and to weigh the pros and cons of each option before deciding to sell.

Many investors see the appeal of real-estate investing as the ease of using financial levereg. There is a chance to buy a property which costs 100 000 EUR with only 20 000 euros of capital. The remainder of the 80000 can be borrowed. This is not an option if you want to buy stocks. However, this option is available. It is possible to get margin loans from your stock portfolio to buy stocks. However, it is more restricted and has higher risk. Aside from that, this logic is pretty opposite. First, your portfolio must already contain stocks that you can use to secure the margin loan. The leverage cap is usually 50%. This makes it more appealing for stock traders. Investors can use a greater amount of debt to fund their portfolio. For stock investing to have leverage worth 20 000 to $30 000 euros, one must have at least 100 000 euros in stocks.

However, this type of leverage can be more risky that the one for real estate investments. Because stock prices can fluctuate greatly both intradayly as well as daily, this means that if an investor doesn't comply with the margin requirements, then a part of his stock portfolio is liquidated and sold automatically. For real estate investments, the risk of using leverage is lower and it is much easier to plan, organize, and negotiate the terms of loans. This is the thing that many investors find most appealing about realty investing. This is the reason that you can expect higher long-term returns on your capital. In an environment where interest rate are low, this is especially important.

This is the biggest disadvantage of real estate investment. If you are interested in renting properties, you should at least visit the property occasionally and be ready to repair, modify or redesign it. This requires some skills and time, but it's much easier when you have an interest. Some people have it while others do not. This is subjective, as you can see. This might also apply to stock investment. Some people find it difficult to dig into quarterly and annual accounts. Everything is subjective.

It is important to be creative. First of all we don't need to do everything ourselves. Real estate investing is best done in a group of people with similar interests. This allows us to easily divide tasks and allow us to talk to others when we have to make difficult decisions. It is possible to hire other people to do the work you don't want or enjoy. It could be repairs, cleaning or renovations. However, you must pay for these outsourced services. As an investor, this leaves you with less cash flow or return. Sometimes outsourcing can even cause you to lose profits. There is another way. Alternative ways to include real estate in your investment portfolio that don't require you to deal directly with tenants, broken toilets and renovations.

How Can One Invest into Real Estate?

When we think about investing in real estate, our first thought is to buy a property. A property that is rented out to others, such as an apartment or house. This strategy comes with some disadvantages. One drawback is that this strategy can take a lot time. First we need to locate a suitable property. After that, we will have to negotiate terms, arrange financing and make the transaction. If necessary, we will then need to find tenants. It is possible to outsource certain or all of these things but it will reduce our returns.

One more thing to take into account when calculating the profitability of potential rental properties. There is one more aspect to consider when calculating profitability for a potential rental property. It is vacancy. This is something novice investors in real estate tend to overlook. Vacancy creates uncertainty for cash flows. Also, it takes effort to find a suitable tenant every time it occurs. One thing that many people find difficult is the fact that investing in real estate requires a lot of money. A mortgage or bank loan may not be able to finance 80%, but it will still allow the investor to pay the 20% down payment.

What can one do with that little capital? Or that much spare time? Or an interest to be involved in every phase of the process. Is there any other way to invest in property?

This list is not complete and does not include all possible options. Each option comes with its own pros, and cons. Some of them could be considered investment in real estate, while others can be described as hustling. For example, you can rent out a room on a daily or weekly basis from your own house. A property can be purchased or you can take part in the ownership of a property that's located in a popular area. Flipping allows you to purchase a property and renovate or redesign it before selling it. We have seen an increase in crowdfunding platforms in recent years. These platforms let investors lend their funds to real property development companies or loan it out for a finished property. It's possible to get many versions or alterations.

To top it all, there is an additional way to get involved in the expected rises of real property prices. This is earning a small portion of the rental income a property generates. This involves investing in real property using investment funds. Real

Estate Investment Trusts and REITs are examples.

Conclusion

This book can be a legal document that helps you achieve your estate planning goals. Trusts can contain many assets, of various values. This allows for ease and comfort in the process of transferring these assets to your estate. Your property can be governed by a Last Will. This will save you the expensive probate costs and fees.

Everyone should look into a Living Trust. But it is particularly recommended for seniors and individuals who are approaching retirement. No matter what size your estate may be, estate planning should be considered. It is important to review your Estate plan whenever you experience a major life change, such a marriage, child birth, or death. A Last Will and Testament can be used to transfer your property once you have passed away. It is simple, straightforward, well-known, widely accepted, and easy to use. Living Trusts are an important tool that you should research and consider. This could be the best option for you to realize all your goals.

www.ingramcontent.com/pod-product-compliance
Lightning Source LLC
Chambersburg PA
CBHW071648210326
41597CB00017B/2151